It's Hot, Hot, Hot!
A Kid's Guide To Hawaiian Volcanoes National Park

Photography by John D. Weigand
Poetry by Penelope Dyan

Bellissima Publishing, LLC
Jamul, California
www.bellissimapublishing.com

Copyright © 2013 by Penny D. Weigand and John D. Weigand

All rights reserved. No part of this book may be reproduced or transmitted in any form or by any means, electronic or mechanical, including photocopying, recording, or by any other means, or by any information or storage retrieval system, without permission from the publisher.

ISBN 978-1-61477-118-0
First Edition

Volcanoes do more than just light up your life, they make our world a bigger place!

Penelope Dyan

It's Hot, Hot, Hot!
Bellissima Publishing, LLC

Introduction

The island of Hawai'i, the largest of the Hawaiian Islands, was formed by a total of six volcanoes, including the submerged Mahukona Volcano off the northwest shore of the 'Big Island of Hawaii,' and five more volcanoes above sea level: Mauna Kea, Mauna Loa, Kohala, Hualālai and Kilauea. Kilauea Volcano is currently the most active volcano on earth, and Kilauea has covered more than 500 square miles of Hawaii with lava in the last 1,100 years, and we are still counting those square miles, because Kilauea has been actively erupting e since 1983. The Kīlauea and Mauna Loa Volcanoes are considered active, The Mauna Kea, Hualālai and Haleakalā volcanoes are dormant, but not extinct. The other volcanoes in the Hawaiian Islands are believed to be completely extinct.

Take a look at some of what award winning author, attorney and former teacher, Penelope Dyan, and photographer John D. Weigand saw as they went in search of the Kilauea Volcano, from their stop at the Kilauea Visitor Center to the mist, the rainbow and the fiery volcanic night! Watch a music video on the Bellissimavideo YouTube Channel, and make your very own volcano! And remember this is also a learn to read book, filled with repetition, word recognition and rhyme!

It's Hot, Hot, Hot!
Bellissima Publishing, LLC

It's Hot, Hot, Hot!
A Kid's Guide To Hawaiian Volcanoes National Park

Photography by John D. Weigand
Poetry by Penelope Dyan

When you get to Volcano Park
the visitor center is where
you should go.
You will find a friendly
park ranger inside,
and he'll tell you everything
that you'll need to know.

There is a sign up the street
that leads to where
the earth lets off some steam.

Steam Vents

←

400 FEET

And when you get to that spot,
if feels just like a dream.

You watch the steam rise.
You see grass and flowers growing.
You marvel at the sight of it
without really knowing,
from where the steam comes,
and why is it so,
that here in the rising hot steam
the grass and flowers grow.

You go for lunch
and there is a rain forest nearby.
Your mom says,
"That is so beautiful,
that I just want to cry."

And because there is a rain forest,
there is a mist in the air,
and as the cauldron smokes,
a rainbow appears RIGHT there!
You wonder if it is really true
(as you have been told)
that at the rainbow's end
is a green leprechaun
guarding a pot full of gold!

If you look closely you can see
where there is a crater
there in the earth--
It is from this crater's volcano
and five other volcanoes,
that this 'Big Island'
was given its birth.

It's bubble, bubble, but
not toil and trouble.
This is NOT a witch's brew.
Your mother becomes
a little nervous,
but Dad says watching
from so far away,
is a VERY safe thing to do.

The sun darkens in the sky,
and at that very moment you know,
that soon you will see
something quite special,
a red and a fiery show.

And as the yellow-orange sun
settles against the sky of blue,
you wonder what sights
await deep in the night for you.

And then . . . finally there it is,
a yellow and red plume of fire!
It is moving up in the sky!
It goes higher and higher and higher!
You are standing high up on a ledge,
and you're away from the heat.
You look up at your dad.
Then you look down at your feet.
You realize that
when it comes to creation
(after all)
God is great, and we are small.

Make Your Own Volcano--Outdoors!
(Much better For Mom Than The Indoor kind)

1 tablespoon of liquid dish-washing soap
3 drops of red food coloring (or more as you like)
1 cup of vinegar
1 1/4 cups of warm water
2 heaping tablespoons of baking soda
1 empty 20 oz. plastic bottle
A bunch of dirt

Directions: Be sure to get permission & do not try without adult supervision

1. Get ready to build a mountain of dirt up around the 20 oz plastic bottle. We dug a hole to make it easier.

2. Combine the soap, food coloring, water and vinegar in the bottle and put on the lid, so dirt won't fall into the bottle when you make your mountain. The liquid should be almost to the top.

3. Build a kid sized mountain around the bottle.

4. Take the baking soda and with a little water make an elongated ball that will fit through the hole in the bottle. (Pretend it is clay.)

5. Take off the bottle top, drop in the elongated ball and shout, "EUREKA!" and then drop the elongated ball right into the bottle. It will erupt just like a volcano!

"Don't dance on a volcano."

A French Proverb

www.ingramcontent.com/pod-product-compliance
Ingram Content Group UK Ltd.
Pitfield, Milton Keynes, MK11 3LW, UK
UKHW060133240426
12048UKWH00002B/22